PICTURE LIBRARY

CATS

PICTURE LIBRARY
CATS

Norman Barrett

Franklin Watts

London   New York   Sydney   Toronto

© 1990 Franklin Watts Ltd

Franklin Watts Inc
387 Park Avenue South
New York
NY 10016

Designed by
Barrett & Weintroub

Photographs by
Marc Henrie
Norman Barrett

Illustration by
Rhoda & Robert Burns

Technical Consultant
Joan Moore

Library of Congress Cataloging-in-Publication Data

Barrett, Norman S.
    Cats/Norman Barrett.
       p.   cm. — (Picture library)
    Summary: Describes several varieties of cats, their behavior, diet, and roles in domestic and wild
habitats.
    ISBN 0-531-14041-5
    1. Cats—Juvenile literature.   [1. Cats.]   I. Title.
    II. Series.
    SF445.7.B38   1990

                                        89-29347
                                          CIP
                                          AC

Contents

Introduction

Cats are among the most popular pets with people all over the world. They are highly intelligent animals, noted for their beauty and grace of movement.

If treated well as young kittens, household cats grow up to be playful, affectionate pets. They keep themselves clean and are creatures of habit. But each cat has its own individual character.

△ Kittens are playful, cuddly creatures. If treated well, they become friendly family pets.

The cat belongs to the same family as the lion and tiger. And even though cats have been domesticated (tamed) for thousands of years, they still have many of the habits and instincts of wild cats.

They hunt small mammals and birds. They can climb trees, run fast over short distances, and make huge leaps. They also sleep a lot. If left to fend for themselves, most cats could survive in the wild.

△ A cat stalks its prey. Even domestic cats who are well fed have an urge to go hunting.

Looking at cats

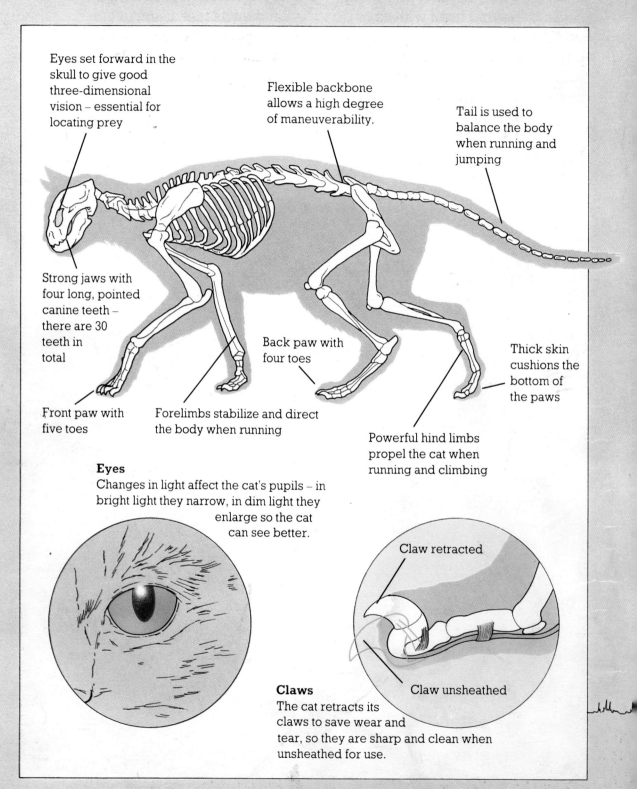

Eyes set forward in the skull to give good three-dimensional vision – essential for locating prey

Flexible backbone allows a high degree of maneuverability.

Tail is used to balance the body when running and jumping

Strong jaws with four long, pointed canine teeth – there are 30 teeth in total

Back paw with four toes

Thick skin cushions the bottom of the paws

Front paw with five toes

Forelimbs stabilize and direct the body when running

Powerful hind limbs propel the cat when running and climbing

Eyes
Changes in light affect the cat's pupils – in bright light they narrow, in dim light they enlarge so the cat can see better.

Claw retracted

Claw unsheathed

Claws
The cat retracts its claws to save wear and tear, so they are sharp and clean when unsheathed for use.

Climbing . . .
A cat climbs by holding on with its claws, steadying itself with its forelimbs and using its hind limbs to push itself up. The cat will descend backwards, turning to jump as it nears the ground.

. . . and falling
A cat can fall from a height and land on its feet, using its exceptional flexibility and balance to turn as it falls. This is known as the "righting reflex."

Behavior

The habits of cats are well known and there for all to see. But the reasons for certain cat behavior are not always obvious and are often misunderstood.

We have all seen a cat sharpening its claws — on a carpet or chair, or outdoors on a wooden post. But it is not so well known that the cat is stripping off its worn-out claw sheaths. On its hind feet, it does this by chewing the sheaths off.

△ A cat claws at a wooden roof with its front paws. It does this for exercise and to shed the outer casing of its claws. The action also has the effect of releasing scent from glands on the underside of the paws. This is called scent-marking.

△ A cat stands guard over its territory. The size of a domestic cat's territory depends on the number of cats in the neighborhood.

▷ A tom (male) cat sprays urine onto bushes. This is to mark its territory, by leaving its scent, or smell, there. This serves as a message or a warning to other cats.

You can tell a cat's feelings from its body language — its actions and the way it "signals" with parts of its body, such as its tail and ears.

A cat's vocal sounds are also signals. It will attract attention, if it wants to be let out, say, by meowing. A contented cat purrs. But a cat in pain might also purr. This is thought to be a plea for friendship or help.

△ Arching of the back signals aggression or fear, or both. This action also involves stretching the legs, bristling the fur and standing sideways towards the cause of the fright. Such a display, often accompanied by hissing, makes the cat look much bigger.

A cat wags its tail when it is angry. But tail movements might also mean that the cat cannot decide what to do.

When a cat's ears are held straight up and slightly forward, it is a sign of a good mood. When the openings point forward, it is alert. An aggressive cat first turns its ears back and down, and then forward when it attacks. The ears of a defensive or frightened cat are completely flattened.

▽ A cat greets one of its "family" by rubbing up against her leg. This is more than just friendly contact. The cat is marking the human with scent from the glands of its face, and collecting human scent on its fur, which it may then lick.

△ Cats not only wash themselves, friendly cats also wash each other. Cats lick themselves to smooth their fur as well as to keep clean.

◁ Cats are generally clean animals, and cover up their mess with earth. Unless they are scent-marking, they prefer to cover up their strong personal odors.

△ Time for an
afternoon nap! Cats
sleep for about 16 hours
in a 24-hour period.

▷ Cats sleep almost
anywhere and in the
most extraordinary
positions.

Birth and growing up

Cats can begin mating before they are a year old. The queen (female) is pregnant for about nine weeks before giving birth. On average, cats have three to five kittens at a time, although litters of more than 10 have been known.

A kitten's eyes do not open for up to a week after birth. After about two weeks, their ears open up and their first teeth begin to appear.

△ Kittens drink their mother's milk for about the first four weeks.

After about three weeks, kittens start to walk and to explore their little world. They are curious and enjoy climbing. Their mother takes care of them for about the first six weeks, and often has to rescue them from trouble.

▽ When they have developed their first set of teeth, after about four weeks, kittens can begin to eat solid food and lap water.

Kittens learn from their mother and from playing with each other. After about four weeks, they may be very gently handled.

Kittens should be at least 10 weeks old before being separated from their mother. It is better to allow all the kittens in a litter to stay with their mother for as long as possible. Most cats are fully grown after about a year.

△ Mother cats have to be very patient with kittens who are full of mischief and energy, but sometimes they have to let the little one know who's boss!

▷ However tiny they are, kittens are fond of climbing. It's a mother's job to make sure they come to no harm.

◁ When a kitten wanders too far, mother's there to carry it back to safety. Gripping it by the fold of skin at the back of the neck is quite painless.

19

Kinds of cats

Cats vary in color and in such characteristics as the length of their hair and the shape of their ears. Cat breeders develop a particular breed by mating animals with distinctive features.

Cats that do not belong to a particular breed are called crossbreeds or non-pedigree cats.

▷ A white Longhair. Longhairs, also called Persians, have long, silky fur, small ears and short, bushy tails.

▽ Non-pedigree kittens — just as lovely as any of the special breeds. The two on the left are tortoiseshell and white, the one on the right is red tabby and white.

△ A seal-point Birman (top left) and a tabby-point Siamese (top right). Pointed cats have white or cream coats with points of a different color. The points are the face, ears, feet and tail. The ancestors of the Birmans are said to have guarded the temples of Burma.

◁ A Burmese kitten. Unlike the Birmans, Burmese cats are short-haired.

△ A blue-point Siamese (top right) and a Devon Rex kitten (top left). Wide-eyed and pixie-faced, Rex cats have rippled fur. Siamese are one of the most popular short-haired cats, noted for their bright blue eyes.

▷ The Maine Coon is a gentle breed, so-called because its fur looks like a raccoon's coat.

△ A chocolate Self-Longhair. "Self" means that the cat's fur has a single overall color.

◁ A Manx cat has no tail. Long back legs give it a rabbit-like walk. The lack of a tail does not appear to affect its balance when climbing.

Wild cats

The small, wild members of the cat family are usually known as wild cats. They live in many parts of the world, and include the lynx, bobcat, serval and margay.

Many of these small wild cats look like the domestic cat. But they are larger and stronger and may be dangerous if approached in the wild. They prowl mainly at night, hunting for small mammals and birds.

▽ Geoffroy's cat is a small wild cat similar in appearance to the domestic spotted tabby. It lives in South America and hides in the lower branches of trees, waiting to ambush its prey.

Cats as pets

Cats make wonderful pets. They are loving animals and do not require constant attention. But they rely on their owners for shelter and food and a certain amount of health care.

Owners are responsible for training kittens, making sure they have clean habits. Most cats need extra grooming with a brush or comb to remove loose hairs. They also need veterinary care — vaccinations against disease and treatment for illness or injury.

▽ Cats can live indoors all the time, but some like to go in and out of the house themselves. Most cats can be trained to use a cat flap.

△ Cats should be
supported from below
when held (top right).
To hold a cat immobile
(above), it can be
grasped by the fold of
skin at its neck. An adult
cat should be supported
from below, too, either
by a hand or on a firm
surface.

▷ This sort of behavior
must be stopped at an
early age. A sharp "no"
and its swift removal
from the drape will
teach a kitten the rules.

The story of cats

The first cats

Cats belong to the family Felidae. It is thought that the first members of this family began to appear about 40 million years ago.

Taming cats

Cats were first tamed thousands of years ago. Domestic cats are believed to be descended from the African wild cat, tamed by the ancient Egyptians possibly 5,500 years ago. But the first direct evidence of cats being tamed dates back to 1600 BC in Egypt, nearly 3,600 years ago.

The Egyptians tamed cats to protect their farms and storehouses from rats and mice and even small snakes. They used them for retrieving game when hunting, and soon began to treat the cats as pets.

△ The Egyptian goddess Bastet (left) had the head of a cat and body of a woman. A mummified cat (right) from about 2,800 years ago.

Worshiping cats

Cats became very pampered and were often represented in Egyptian art — sculptures and paintings. They came to be treated as sacred. Serious punishments were introduced for harming cats. A person killing a cat could be sentenced to death.

The Egyptian sun god Ra was often represented as a cat. The Egyptians also worshipped a goddess of love called Bastet, or Bast, who was represented as a cat or having the head of a cat.

△ An ancient Egyptian wall painting shows a master hunting with his cat in the marshes. The Egyptians taught cats to act as retrievers to bring back the dead birds.

The spread of cats

Cats were prized in ancient Greece and Rome for their ability to keep the rodent population down. They were useful for the same purpose on ships. Traders probably took cats to Europe and the Middle East.

A symbol of evil

In the Middle Ages in Europe, cats began to be associated with witches. They became a symbol of evil and thousands were killed. This is thought to be one reason for the spread of the "black death," a plague carried by rats that killed a quarter of Europe's population in the 1300s.

Back in favor

Cats had come back into favor — as pets and rat-catchers — by the 1600s. Colonists from Europe took them to the Americas, where their value in keeping farms and settlements free from rodents was quickly appreciated.

Cat shows

The first cat show was held in July 1871, at the Crystal Palace in London, and 170 cats took part. It attracted much interest from abroad, and the idea soon spread around the world.

△ Big cat shows have 2,000 or more entrants.

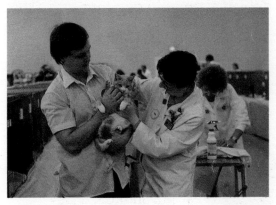

△ Judging at a cat show.

△ The Cymric is a long-haired variety of the tailless Manx, bred in North America in the 1960s. New breeds are constantly being developed.

Facts and records

Swimming cats

Most cats avoid rain and do not like water. But they can swim if necessary. Van cats, a Turkish breed, enjoy swimming, and some rex-coated cats are happy in the water.

△ Van cats are strong swimmers.

Cat colonies

Cats left to take care of themselves can usually survive. They catch rats and mice, drink water from puddles, and beg scraps from passers-by.

Domestic cats that have reverted to the wild are called feral cats. They are often to be found in colonies in such places as docks or old ruins and monuments. Some feral colonies consist of a hundred or more cats and kittens. They rarely fight among themselves.

△ A group of feral cats.

Age

A healthy male cat can expect to live for 12 to 15 years, female cats a year or two longer. But many cats reach the age of 20, and a few have been known to live more than 30 years.

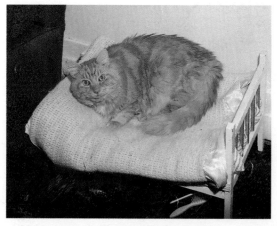

△ An elderly cat of 21 years.

Glossary

Birman
A long-haired breed that originated in Burma, but which is not related to the Burmese.

Burmese
A short-haired breed developed from a cat brought from Burma to the United States in 1930.

Domesticated
Tamed. Domesticated cats have been tame for thousands of years. If left to live in the wild, they are called feral cats.

Non-pedigree cats
Cats of no particular breed, also called crossbreeds.

Pedigree
A pure breed recognized for showing purposes.

Persian
A term sometimes used for Longhair breeds of cat.

Pointed
Having a coat with parts (points) of a different color from that of the main body; the points are the mask (front of the face), ears, feet and tail.

Queen
A female cat.

Rex
A type of cat with rippled fur.

Scent marking
Releasing scent from glands in various parts of the cat's body in order to let other cats know of its presence.

Self-colored
Having a coat of a single color.

Siamese
A popular short-haired breed, with dark points and bright blue eyes, known for its mournful cries when it wants attention.

Tabby
A coat color with patterns of dark stripes and blotches on a lighter background.

Tom
A male cat.

Tortoiseshell
A patched or mottled orange- and-black patterned coat color.

Wild cats
Small members of the cat family that live in the wild.

Index